KEEP
CALM
AND
PASS
YOUR
MUSIC
EXAM

CHESTER MUSIC
part of The Music Sales Group

London/New York/Paris/Sydney/Copenhagen/Berlin/Madrid/Hong Kong/Tokyo

About the author

Charlotte Tomlinson is an internationally recognised expert in performance anxiety. She works primarily as a performance coach, helping musicians to perform at their peak on stage and to express the music in the best way they can. Her approach has been developed largely from her own experience of teaching and performing as a classical pianist.

Based in Oxford, where she teaches piano and chamber music to students from the University of Oxford, her work regularly takes her abroad. She gives talks, masterclasses and performance coaching for conservatoires, universities and festivals around the world, including *Yale Summer School of Music*, the *Verbier Academy* and *Verbier Festival Orchestras*, the *Imani Wind Festival* in New York, the Royal Northern College of Music, the Royal Conservatoire of Scotland, The University of Oxford and the University of Cambridge.

She holds international piano masterclasses every year in Germany, and gives regular workshops for piano teachers on freedom in piano technique. She is passionate about coaching musicians to have greater body awareness when playing and about helping them to avoid unnecessary tension and injury.

She has been interviewed for the BBC's *Proms Extra*, Radio 3's *Music Matters*, the BBC World Service and for the American documentary *Composed*. She has written many articles for national and international music magazines and has conducted a series of interviews with concert musicians about how they manage performance stress, which can be viewed at www.beyondstagefright.com.

www.charlottetomlinson.com

Published by
Chester Music Limited
14-15 Berners Street, London W1T 3LJ, UK.

Exclusive Distributors:

Music Sales Limited
Distribution Centre, Newmarket Road,
Bury St Edmunds, Suffolk IP33 3YB, UK.

Music Sales Corporation
180 Madison Avenue, 24th Floor,
New York NY 10016, USA.

Music Sales Pty Limited
4th floor, Lisgar House, 30-32 Carrington Street,
Sydney, NSW 2000, Australia.

Order No. CH85129
ISBN: 978-1-78558-352-0
This book © Copyright 2017 Wise Publications,
a division of Music Sales Limited.

Illustrations by Joanna Hegemann.
Cover design by Tim Field.
Edited by Thomas Lydon.

The author would like to thank
the many teachers and performers
who lent their expertise to pages 51–55.

Printed in the EU.

www.musicsales.com

INTRODUCTION:

ABOUT THIS BOOK

In this book, we will look at how you can manage your nerves in a number of different ways:

◆ How you deal with the physical symptoms of nerves so that you can work them in your favour

◆ How to manage your Inner Critic when it rears its ugly head

◆ How you prepare, so that you feel secure when you're in your exam

◆ How to manage the exam itself so you can give yourself the very best chance.

CHAPTER 1:

GETTING TO KNOW YOURSELF

Nerves: they are more common than you think

You have a performance exam coming up. How do you feel about it?

If it makes you feel nervous, then you should know that you're not alone. Almost all performers experience nerves of some sort before they play in front of others.

You may think that professionals are above being nervous, but no, they get nervous too. They have just become very skilled at managing their nerves and not letting them show. They are also masters of preparation and have a lot of performing experience, which are two very good ways of keeping nerves manageable.

How do *your* nerves show themselves?

Have a think about how you get nervous. Do you have sweaty hands or a dry mouth? Do you feel faint? Do you shake or do you just feel wobbly emotionally? Do you lack confidence, or feel self-conscious?

The nerves people experience are as individual as the people themselves. You might find that a friend experiences nerves in the same way as you, or you might find that you are polar opposites. It doesn't really matter. The important thing is that you know how your nerves show themselves and what you can do to help yourself when they come up.

"If you know your own body, you can use adrenaline to your advantage"

Adrenaline: make it your friend, not your enemy

Have you ever come across the 'fight-or-flight' response? When this response takes hold, it means that on some level, your body thinks it is dealing with a serious threat to your life and wellbeing.

All sorts of physical changes take place to help you either fight or run from this serious threat:

◆ Adrenaline pumps round your body; your heartbeat gets faster

◆ Blood drains from where it's not so needed (your face or your hands) to your muscles

◆ Your digestion slows down.

Everything is heightened to help you deal with the situation. This is invaluable when you really are in danger, but not when it comes to performing. No performer wants to shake so much that they have no real control over their bow, or have such a racing heartbeat that they can't focus on the task at hand. Nor does any performer want that horrible feeling of wanting the ground to swallow them up or the desperate need to run away from a performance.

These are out-of-control nerves, horrible to deal with and they can really get in the way of a good performance. The good news is that the adrenaline, which is there to help you fight, or run from something seriously scary, can be used to help you.

Adrenaline heightens everything. It keeps you alert and ready to go – but you need the right amount. Too much leads to the out-of-control nerves that get in the way and are horrible to experience; too little and there is no difference between the exam and your practice room.

When you have the right amount, you might have butterflies of excitement in your stomach; you might feel slightly shaky but in a way you can handle; you might even start looking forward to the exam!

It's how you see this adrenaline that's important.
Think about the people who do sports like sky-diving or bungee jumping. They are putting themselves in real danger. So why do they do it? They do it because they love the feeling of that adrenaline pumping round their body. They associate it with fun, excitement and a challenge, otherwise they wouldn't do those sports in the first place.

"It's how you use adrenaline that's important – associate it with fun, excitement and challenge"

You can make this choice too. You can change that adrenaline from being terrifying to being exciting. It can become your friend, not your enemy.

CHAPTER 2:

CALMING YOUR YOUR INNER CRITIC

Who and what is the Inner Critic?

The Inner Critic is a part of yourself that just loves beating you up and telling you that you're no good. It is critical in a negative, emotional and judgmental way. It really loves it when you fail, and it does everything in its power to trip you up. A lot of people think that you need an Inner Critic so that you can play or sing well, but this isn't true. It actually causes havoc and damages everything you do.

Now of course you need feedback of some sort in order to play music well and to reach high standards. But what you don't need is for that feedback to be nasty and bullying. You need feedback that is more objective, less emotional and less judgmental. You need to discern what is good and what is less good about your playing, so that you can improve.

When the Inner Critic pulls the strings

The Inner Critic is a part of you that is overly negative and critical. It loves to beat you up and give you a hard time. It doesn't care about you and it isn't thinking about your overall wellbeing. It is an elusive character and can be clever and manipulative, letting you think that being negatively critical and judgmental is what you need in order to perform well. But once you notice your own Inner Critic, the control it has over you starts to disappear. You start to see it as it really is: one big bully. And bullies are all cowards underneath, once you start to see through the scary image they put across.

The Inner Critic and nerves: one big disaster zone

If the Inner Critic starts getting out of hand, it can badly affect your nerves and stop you performing at your best. When you feel criticised or judged, you will shut right down in order to protect yourself. Anyone would. It's totally normal. And by shutting down, you might be getting:

◆ Physically tense: a bit like putting on armour to make sure that arrows don't get through

◆ Emotionally tense: you might just feel bad about yourself.

Both of these effects will mean that you find it harder to perform, or for that matter, to excel in any way at all. Just imagine, right now, that someone is telling you that you're a really bad musician, that you haven't practised enough and that you're going to fail your exam as a result. How would you feel? Horrible! Nobody wants to hear anything like this. Here are the problems with feedback like this:

◆ It is extremely unlikely that you are a really bad musician

◆ It won't help.

Can you imagine saying all of this to a close friend?
You wouldn't, but you are very likely to say this to yourself
and not think anything of it. You might even think that this
is the best way to do well.

Let's think about the exam for a minute. Imagine that your
Inner Critic is going wild and telling you that you can't do
anything right and that you're bound to do really badly.
You don't feel safe at all and your nerves are going crazy.

If your Inner Critic tells you that you are going to do badly, you will assume that everybody else thinks the same. Your teacher might be trying desperately to reassure you that you're doing fine, but you can't hear because the Inner Critic has got the upper hand. And of course when it comes to the exam, you automatically assume that the examiner must think the same.

The Objective Observer

So what can you do about the Inner Critic once you've noticed it? You need to find a way to practise and perform to your highest standards without beating yourself up and whipping up your nerves. Let's bring in another character: the Objective Observer. The Objective Observer is a part of you that observes what needs to be done and will suggest it in a straightforward, non-judgmental and unemotional way. It is objective, and therefore much kinder.

The Inner Critic might say: 'You're so stupid. How can you get that wrong again? You're always making mistakes. You'll never get any better. You'll fail the exam at this rate. Oh just get it right, you idiot!'

The Objective Observer might say: 'Whoops, that was a slip. What can we do to get that better? Perhaps it needs a better fingering, or better breathing. How about trying this out? Oh, good, that's better. Just make a note of this passage – it needs a little bit more practice to get it really secure.'

Practising with the Objective Observer

Practice isn't just about practising your instrument and practising the music. It applies to anything you want to achieve, and in this case, it is just as important to practice the Objective Observer's approach. You can do this in a few steps. Start by noticing when the Inner Critic kicks in and congratulate yourself for noticing it. Then, press the pause button on that inner dialogue.

Now, give yourself an alternative. Find a non-judgmental, unemotional and straightforward way of looking at the same issue.

Remember that this needs to be practised, and if you can start building this in during your practice time, it is likely to have built itself in firmly by the time you do your exam. It opens up the possibility for all sorts of amazing things to happen as a result.

Here are the kinds of things that can happen when the Objective Observer starts being embedded:

◆ You slip up in the exam but you find your place quickly, and you don't get upset about it

◆ The examiner has a bit of a scowl on his or her face, but you don't think it's because of you or how you're playing. The reality might be that they're a bit tired and their smile muscles have got tired too

◆ You find that actually you're not that nervous. You have a few butterflies perhaps, but that's more like excitement. You can't quite believe it, but you're secretly rather looking forward to the exam.

"Notice when the Inner Critic kicks in, and press the pause button"

Be aware that the Objective Observer does not sugar-coat their comments. They do not say, 'That was brilliant, wonderful, fantastic!' without saying why. They are there to help you. Being 'objective', they know not to give you a false sense of security, but to be realistic and supportive.

Chill out!

Sometimes the Inner Critic will pop up when you're least expecting it. Let's say you've done really well to employ the Objective Observer's approach but the Inner Critic has found a way in through the back door.

Don't fight it. It usually doesn't help much. The Inner Critic will just argue the case and come back with all sorts of reasons, which you might start believing if you're not careful. Just have a bit of a laugh and say to yourself: 'There it goes again, trying to get me down. Oh well, that's ok. I'm just not going to give it the time of day. I can just chill out and not worry. I've got other ways of doing things now.'

And with that, you remind yourself of the Objective Observer again, finding your confidence and feeling good.

"You don't
need to
    fight your
Inner Critic,
    you can
simply
    ignore it!"

CHAPTER 3:

PRACTISING EFFECTIVELY

It's entirely possible that you don't actually know what practising is. That's quite a statement, but take time to think about this for a minute. Are you sure that you know what you need to do in order to get your playing up to a level where you can rely on it?

Practising efficiently is a good way to help you keep your nerves under control. If you ask a professional musician what the one thing is that would make them really nervous for a performance, they will all say, 'not being prepared'. Some would even say that if you're not prepared, you're asking for your nerves to kick in. Then apply this to yourself and imagine doing your exam and not being prepared. It's enough to make your heart beat go through the roof.

What is practising?

Let's think of practising for your exam as being like an iceberg.

The tip of the iceberg is the exam itself and the rest of it is the practising you need to do for the exam. As you can see, most of the iceberg, the invisible part under the water, is much bigger than the tip of the iceberg. That is the same with practising. You need to do much, much more practising than you think, disproportionately more, to be secure in a performance.

Quality *and* quantity

So is it just about finding more time to practise? Quite possibly, but it's also about being efficient with the time you spend, so that you know what you're doing and can be genuinely confident.

"You need to do much, much more practising than you think"

Let's look at a few ways to practise efficiently:

◆ **Give yourself goals:** plan what you want to achieve in each practice time, and check at the end that you've covered everything

◆ **Keep focused:** half an hour of good, efficient practising is way more effective than an hour or more of idling your way through and not achieving much

◆ **Listen to your teacher:** take notice of what they have pointed out, practise exactly that, and see it get better. It's so easy to pay lip service to what someone else has suggested you do, but actually *doing* it can be a revelation. Nice for the teacher, too!

◆ **Mix it up:** if you're someone who tends to put all your focus on the first part of a piece and then ends up being surprised by how little you know the rest of it, why not begin at a different point in the piece? You could even start at the end and work backwards to make sure you're covering everything.

Cramming doesn't work

You can just about cram facts and figures into your head the day before an academic exam, although it is never advisable and not the best way to learn. What you're doing is relying on your short-term memory. Unfortunately, it doesn't work like this in performance exams. In order to feel secure in a performance, you need everything to be built into your long-term memory. Why? Because the adrenaline that pumps around your system as you go into a performance exam can destabilise you if you're not prepared. You will only be able to do what is firmly embedded in your long-term memory.

To achieve this, you need to prepare well in advance and fix a date by which time you will be ready that is *ahead of the exam*.

"When it comes to performance, your long-term memory takes over"

This is now the date by which your pieces, scales and all the components that make up your exam need to be secure and firmly built in. You want all note mistakes to be corrected, all fingerings sorted, breaths organised and all details to be well embedded into your long-term memory.

This will give you the chance to test out how you respond to the pumping adrenaline, before the actual exam itself. This is when you need to practise performing.

Practising performing

In the week or so before the exam, when you feel happy with your preparation, try out your whole exam as many times as you can in front of an audience. Even an audience of one will make a difference. Do it in the exam venue if you can, but if not, somewhere a little bit more official than you're used to. Treat this as a time when you can really learn about yourself. Take the opportunity to learn how you cope under pressure and use the experience to practise keeping yourself focused. Each time you perform, you'll find you get better.

Real performing can only happen when you trust that you have done your preparation – when you are secure and can let go and play. Things start to go wrong when you go into an exam with your practising head on. You think too much about how to play and that's when you want to stop and correct as you go along. Adrenaline has no mercy in these situations and you may find you go blank or feel out of control, with your nerves going crazy.

You need to be so well prepared that the adrenaline supports you, giving you butterflies of excitement, helping you play at your best. If you create the right environment for it, as we have said before, this is when adrenaline can be your friend and not your enemy.

Working with a pianist

If you're working with a pianist, be prepared for this.
Give yourself opportunities to rehearse with them well
in advance.

◆ Get to know what's happening musically: even if you
are comfortable with your own part, everything might
sound different and unfamiliar when playing with
another instrument.

◆ Get to know the pianist as a person: knowing the
person and having a chance to rehearse with them in
advance will help immeasurably. You will feel much
more secure.

"The more time you spend with your pianist, the better"

Visualisation

Visualisation is something we do every day of our lives, although we're mostly not aware of it. Imagine, for example, that you once you finish reading this chapter, you decide you're going to have a drink. You will probably see in your mind's eye what drink you want, you might even imagine tasting it or hearing the sound of the mug or glass as the drink is poured into it. What we're really talking about here is imagining and sensing something in advance, whether it's seeing it, hearing it, feeling it or tasting it.

Now we're going to use this more consciously. Try spending the last few minutes of your practice time *imagining* you're doing your exam. It will get you used to the feeling of dealing with some nervous energy and you will quickly realise which parts of your performance need work. Don't worry if you feel a bit anxious; it is still a useful practice tool because you can address any problems in the safety of your own practice room.

Now do the same exercise again and imagine the exam going really well.

Can you imagine feeling really confident and secure, walking into the room to play, looking forward to playing, with a few butterflies of excitement? This can be very powerful; your unconscious mind doesn't know the difference between imagination and reality, and the process of visualisation can have a massive impact on your actual performance.

A little caveat here: if you find you can't easily imagine the exam going well, stop for the time being, and wait until you can find some more positive feelings. There is no point in compounding the negative ones. Once you are feeling better, then just go for it.

CHAPTER 4:

NAILING THE EXAM

Fake it 'til you make it

In the last chapter we talked about visualisation and how your unconscious mind doesn't know the difference between imagination and reality. Well, you can really use this to your advantage on the actual day of the exam. You can just do a little bit of acting until you start feeling really confident.

The 'Yessss!' feeling

Think about an athlete winning a race. They throw their arms up wide and what they're saying through their body language is, 'Yes! I've done it – I've won!' Give this a go yourself and see what it feels like. Stand up really tall, with your feet flat on the ground, hip-width apart and throw your arms up in the air as if you're that winning athlete.

Say 'Yessss!' either out loud, or if this feels a little uncomfortable you can say it in your head. What you're saying through your body language is, 'Yes, I can do it! Yes, I can do this exam. It's going to be really good.' Now check in to see what this feels like. You might feel a little bit odd or self-conscious at first, so maybe try it a few times until you really get that good feeling going.

Then see what happens if you keep your arms up in the 'Yessss!' pose for longer, perhaps for about a minute. A minute is quite a long time when you're doing something like this, so look at a clock if you need to. What this is doing for you is getting you to feel good. When you feel good about doing an exam, you are likely to enjoy it and there is a strong chance that you will do better.

Walk tall

Now you can take the 'Yesss!' feeling, stand up straight and start walking. Imagine you are taller than you really are. Feel as if something is pulling your head upwards towards the ceiling. If you are small for your age, it's fun to pretend you're taller. If you are tall for your age, the likelihood is you might be slouching as you walk, so just pretend you are *even* taller – and that you're proud of it! Tall people look fantastic when they stand tall and don't slouch. You're fine whatever height you are; this technique can just help you to feel even more confident.

Your exam really starts the moment you walk into the exam room; how you come into the room makes a big difference to how the exam goes. The examiner might not be aware of this consciously, but on some level they *will* be aware and it will make an impact. But much more important than this is how it makes *you* feel, and you just want to feel good.

Smile at the examiner

You may not want to smile at the examiner and you may feel you've got too much to think about to do this, but just do it: smile! This will be wonderful for any examiner.

Who doesn't like to be greeted with a beaming smile? But again, more importantly it is wonderful for you. It gets your endorphins going and those are the chemicals your body makes that make you feel good.

And what about the examiner anyway?

The examiner might be writing a lot while you are playing, but don't be put off by this. They have a lot to do in a short amount of time, but they really will be listening to you. They are likely to be very friendly and encouraging, but perhaps, once in a blue moon they may not be, or maybe you *feel* that they're not. That's ok, just don't lose your cool and let this put you off. Think instead of how much you've prepared and how ready you are to do this exam. Whoever the examiner is, they will love it when you play or sing well. It will make their day.

"Don't let the examiner put you off; they will be rooting for you"

Exam day checklist

Everyone:

◆ Remember your music!

◆ Photocopies are not usually allowed in Grade exams except to facilitate a difficult page turn – you should check the rules issued by the board in question.

String players:

◆ Make sure you have clean strings (but use a dry duster only on exam day)

◆ Put just the right amount of rosin on your bow

◆ Check rosin and bow hair tension with long, slow bows. This can also help to calm nerves

◆ Tune before *and* when you go into the exam room, and re-tune whenever you need to

◆ Check the string adjusters have enough space to move effectively, otherwise adjust with the peg first

◆ Cello and basses: make sure your stool is at the right height

◆ Spike holders and slip mats need to be absolutely secure.

Singers:

◆ Bring a water bottle in with you to counteract a dry mouth, which can happen if you're nervous

◆ Make sure that you can see your pianist

◆ To prepare, hum through the songs with dynamics and then talk through the lyrics, feeling the feelings you are putting into the song.

◆ Wearing heels affects your stance and stability – wearing flat shoes might be better, especially if you get wobbly knees when you're nervous

Woodwind players:

◆ Make sure you have a played-in extra reed with you (oboe/bassoon/clarinet)

◆ Take in water if you need it – and remember to take it out again!

◆ Bassoonists: make sure you have a comfortable chair. Ask for a straight-backed, flat-bottomed chair if you need to

◆ Make sure you adjust the height of the stand

◆ Take a cleaning cloth in with you

◆ Clarinettists: if you have to play B♭ and A clarinet in the exam, keep your A barrel in your pocket so it's nicely warmed up before you play.

Brass players:

◆ Check that your valves are oiled and slides greased and moving smoothly, and empty your instrument of any condensation before you go into the exam room. Remember that it is fine to empty out again during your exam, perhaps between pieces. The examiner will know that this is perfectly normal

◆ Alongside your usual warmup routine, you can:
  • Buzz on the mouthpiece
  • Play on the mouthpiece only
  • Play long notes, breathing deeply from the diaphragm, gradually extending the length each time. This also helps to control nerves!

◆ If you can't warm up with a full open sound because of disturbance to other candidates, then use a mute or practice mute

◆ Some people benefit from a lighter practice session on the day before the exam, with a heavier session the day before that. Find out what works best for you

◆ Remember: only by breathing properly, deeply and in a relaxed manor can you achieve your best sound, range and endurance.

Pianists:

◆ Adjust the piano stool to the height that is right for you

◆ Check you can turn your pages comfortably and make sure you have practised any awkward turns well in advance

◆ Take a tissue in with you if you have sweaty hands

◆ Anyone wearing heels: be aware that they can affect your pedalling and how you sit at the piano.

Remember to support yourself physically

What do you need on the day of a performance? Do you need to eat beforehand to give yourself energy? Do you need to be quiet just before the exam or does chatting make you feel better?

Here are a few examples of what you can do to look after yourself physically:

◆ *Energy:* discover whether you need to eat before or after the exam. If you need the energy before, make sure you eat the right food for you. Don't dose up on sugar, because your blood sugar will go sky high for a short period of time and then will crash right back down again – not something you want right in the middle of your exam! Perhaps a little bit of protein to balance the sugar spike in some carbohydrates – a sandwich with meat, fish, cheese or eggs in it. Nuts are a good source of energy, and some musicians swear by bananas because they're easy to digest and give a lot of energy, without being overly sugary

◆ *Hydration:* drinking a glass of water particularly helps woodwind and brass players, along with singers, but it is a good idea for everybody. It is said that being hydrated can help your brain to work more efficiently

◆ *Relaxation:* notice if you feel a bit stiff and tense before you perform and do any stretches you can think of to unlock those tight muscles. Just make them up – anything that helps you feel more free and less tight!

Breathe, take time and get comfortable

Breathing is one of the best things you can do when you're nervous. It will calm you right down very quickly. You just need to remember to do it!

Breathe while you're waiting outside the exam room; breathe when you are preparing yourself to perform; and if you start panicking or worrying in the middle of the exam, just find a moment to take a couple of slow, deep breaths. It will help you so much.

When you get into the exam, don't feel pressurised to start straight away. It's your exam and you can take time to feel comfortable.

Take time to adjust the piano stool, the music stand, to tune your instrument – whatever you need – and once you're ready, count to three in your head before you start just to make sure you're not launching headlong into it all.

"Find a moment to take a couple of slow, deep breaths"

Focus

Focus is a very important part of performing. If you practise keeping your focus when you practise and when you are practising performing, you will find it much easier when you come to the exam itself.

Being focused in an activity is intensely satisfying. If you are watching a good movie and are totally involved, you are focused. You may hate being disturbed. If you can be focused in your exam, which means being in the present moment, with all your concentration on the task involved, you will find it a much more enjoyable experience. It has a magical impact on nerves too – they have a tendency to disappear!

When mistakes happen

Mistakes happen! They are part and parcel of live performance. A little inside information here: they happen to everybody, including professionals. Yes, really! The only difference between experienced professionals performing and you taking an exam is that the professionals are really skilled at getting back on track if they slip up. They don't let it show. They are also really skilled at practising, so they minimise the possibility of slipping up by knowing the music inside out. And, of course, they have bags of performing experience, so they know what they're dealing with; they are familiar with being on stage.

Just look at those words for a second. They are 'skilled' at dealing with performance. Skilled means that they have learnt a skill – they have *practised* performing so they get good at managing slip-ups in live performance. That means that you can learn that skill too. You can get really good at managing mistakes and getting back on track.

The first step when you make a mistake is to *just keep going*. Find your place back in the music, or scale or whatever it is, as quickly as possible and carry on as if nothing has happened. Don't let yourself slide down the slippery slope of despair because of one measly mistake. That will just encourage more and more mistakes, which isn't what you want. If that Inner Critic comes back and gives you a hard time, just tell it to *chill out* and explain that you're in charge here!

If you stop mid-performance and have a blank, and you can't find your way back, ask the examiner if you can start the piece or the scale again, and take your time. There is no hurry. And breathe, breathe, breathe. This will calm you right down and give you the best possible chance. Many musicians have had crazy disasters happen on stage and have still carried on to give a great performance – and you can too!

A fun adventure

It might seem a bit crazy to you to see an exam as a fun adventure, but if you can, you will find it all becomes so much easier and more enjoyable. What an exam gives you is an opportunity to learn all sorts of new skills and build up your ability. It gives you a chance to learn about practising and performing. It gives you an opportunity to focus all those skills in a short period of time.

An exam is a snapshot, a moment in time when you show what you can do. It can be quite useful in that way. But it doesn't and shouldn't sum you up as a musician. It shows *where* you are but not *who* you are. You are more than your exam.

> "... an exam doesn't and shouldn't sum you up as a musician. It shows you where you are, but not who you are"

You did it!

You have done your exam and it went by in a flash. Some things went well and some things didn't. Now is the time to let go. Make sure your Inner Critic doesn't come back to haunt you. Watch that you don't focus on the one mistake you made, forgetting all the other good things you've done. You've done the best you can, even if the Inner Critic says you haven't.

Let go. It's all out of your hands now. You may get a high mark or you may not. A high mark is always nice and a lower mark is a bit more of a challenge to deal with. But you've done your best, you've learnt loads and fingers crossed, you've enjoyed the whole thing. And that's what all this exam business is about!